Jocoseria by Robert Browning

Robert Browning is one of the most significant Victorian Poets and, of course, English Poetry.

Much of his reputation is based upon his mastery of the dramatic monologue although his talents encompassed verse plays and even a well-regarded essay on Shelley during a long and prolific career.

He was born on May 7th, 1812 in Walmouth, London. Much of his education was home based and Browning was an eclectic and studious student, learning several languages and much else across a myriad of subjects, interests and passions.

Browning's early career began promisingly. The fragment from his intended long poem Pauline brought him to the attention of Dante Gabriel Rossetti, and was followed by Paracelsus, which was praised by both William Wordsworth and Charles Dickens. In 1840 the difficult Sordello, which was seen as willfully obscure, brought his career almost to a standstill.

Despite these artistic and professional difficulties his personal life was about to become immensely fulfilling. He began a relationship with, and then married, the older and better known Elizabeth Barrett. This new foundation served to energise his writings, his life and his career.

During their time in Italy they both wrote much of their best work. With her untimely death in 1861 he returned to London and thereafter began several further major projects.

The collection Dramatis Personae (1864) and the book-length epic poem The Ring and the Book (1868-69) were published and well received; his reputation as a venerated English poet now assured.

Robert Browning died in Venice on December 12th, 1889.

Index of Contents

NOTE

This collection of poems was published in 1883. The title of the volume is mentioned in a foot-note to the Note at the end of Paracelsus, where the poet speaks of "such rubbish as Melander's Jocoseria." In a letter, accompanying a copy of the volume, sent to a friend, Browning wrote: "The title is taken from the work of Melander Schwartzmann, reviewed, by a curious coincidence, in the Blackwood of this month [February, 1883]. I referred to it in a note to Paracelsus. The two Hebrew quotations in the note to Jochanan Hakkadosh put in to give a grave look to what is mere fun and invention being translated amount to (1) 'A Collection of Lies'; and (2), an old saying, 'From Moses to Moses arose none like Moses.'"

WANTING IS—WHAT?

This is in the nature of a prelude to the entire group of poems.

Wanting is—what?
Summer redundant,
Blueness abundant,
—Where is the blot?
Beamy the world, yet a blank all the same,
—Framework which waits for a picture to frame:
What of the leafage, what of the flower?
Roses embowering with naught they embower!
Come then, complete incompletion, O comer,
Pant through the blueness, perfect the summer!
Breathe but one breath
Rose-beauty above,
And all that was death
Grows life, grows love,
Grows love!

DONALD

This story which Browning had from the lips of the hero has also been told in prose by Sir Walter Scott.

"Will you hear my story also,
—Huge Sport, brave adventure in plenty?"
The boys were a band from Oxford,
The oldest of whom was twenty.

The bothy we held carouse in
Was bright with fire and candle;
Tale followed tale like a merry-go-round
Whereof Sport turned the handle.

In our eyes and noses—turf-smoke:
In our ears a tune from the trivet,
Whence "Boiling, boiling," the kettle sang,
"And ready for fresh Glenlivet."

So, feat capped feat, with a vengeance:
Truths, though,—the lads were loyal:
Grouse, five-score brace to the bag!
Deer, ten hours' stalk of the Royal!"

Of boasting, not one bit, boys!
Only there seemed to settle
Somehow above your curly heads,
—Plain through the singing kettle,

Palpable through the cloud,
As each new-puffed Havana
Rewarded the teller's well-told tale,—
This vaunt "To Sport—Hosanna!

"Hunt, fish, shoot,
Would a man fulfil life's duty!
Not to the bodily frame alone
Does Sport give strength and beauty,

"But character gains in—courage?
Ay, Sir, and much beside it!
You don't sport, more 's the pity;
You soon would find, if you tried it,

"Good sportsman means good fellow,
Sound-hearted he, to the centre;
Your mealy-mouthed mild milksops
—There 's where the rot can enter!

"There 's where the dirt will breed,
The shabbiness Sport would banish!
Oh no, Sir, no! In your honored case
All such objections vanish.

"'T is known how hard you studied:
A Double-First—what, the jigger!
Give me but half your Latin and Greek,
I 'll never again touch trigger!

"Still, tastes are tastes, allow me!
Allow, too, where there 's keenness

For Sport, there 's little likelihood
Of a man's displaying meanness!"

So, put on my mettle, I interposed.
"Will you hear my story?" quoth I.
Never mind how long since it happed,
I sat, as we sit, in a bothy;

"With as merry a band of mates, too,
Undergrads all on a level:
(One 's a Bishop, one 's gone to the Bench,
And one's gone—well, to the Devil.)

"When, lo, a scratching and tapping!
In hobbled a ghastly visitor.
Listen to just what he told us himself
—No need of our playing inquisitor!"

Do you happen to know in Ross-shire
Mount Ben ... but the name scarce matters:
Of the naked fact I am sure enough,
Though I clothe it in rags and tatters.

You may recognize Ben by description;
Behind him—a moor's immenseness:
Up goes the middle mount of a range,
Fringed with its firs in denseness.

Rimming the edge, its fir-fringe, mind!
For an edge there is, though narrow;
From end to end of the range, a strip
Of path runs straight as an arrow.

And the mountaineer who takes that path
Saves himself miles of journey
He has to plod if he crosses the moor
Through heather, peat, and burnie.

But a mountaineer he needs must be,
For, look you, right in the middle
Projects bluff Ben—with an end in ich—
Why planted there, is a riddle:

Since all Ben's brothers little and big
Keep rank, set shoulder to shoulder,
And only this burliest out must bulge
Till it seems—to the beholder

From down in the gully,—as if Ben's breast,
To a sudden spike diminished,
Would signify to the boldest foot
"All further passage finished!"

Yet the mountaineer who sidles on
And on to the very bending,
Discovers, if heart and brain be proof,
No necessary ending.

Foot up, foot down, to the turn abrupt
Having trod, he, there arriving,
Finds—what he took for a point was breadth,
A mercy of Nature's contriving.

So, he rounds what, when 't is reached, proves straight,
From one side gains the other:
The wee path widens—resume the march,
And he foils you, Ben my brother!

But Donald—(that name, I hope, will do)—
I wrong him if I call "foiling"
The tramp of the callant, whistling the while
As blithe as our kettle's boiling.

He had dared the danger from boyhood up,
And now,—when perchance was waiting
A lass at the brig below,—'twixt mount
And moor would he stand debating?

Moreover this Donald was twenty-five,
A glory of bone and muscle:
Did a fiend dispute the right of way,
Donald would try a tussle.

Lightsomely marched he out of the broad
On to the narrow and narrow;
A step more, rounding the angular rock,
Reached the front straight as an arrow.

He stepped it, safe on the ledge he stood,
When—whom found he full-facing?
What fellow in courage and wariness too,
Had scouted ignoble pacing,

And left low safety to timid mates,
And made for the dread dear danger,
And gained the height where—who could guess

He would meet with a rival ranger?

'T was a gold-red stag that stood and stared,
Gigantic and magnific,
By the wonder—ay, and the peril—struck
Intelligent and pacific:

For a red deer is no fallow deer
Grown cowardly through park-feeding;
He batters you like a thunderbolt
If you brave his haunts unheeding.

I doubt he could hardly perform volte-face
Had valor advised discretion:
You may walk on a rope, but to turn on a rope
No Blondin makes profession.

Yet Donald must turn, would pride permit,
Though pride ill brooks retiring:
Each eyed each—mute man, motionless beast—
Less fearing than admiring.

These are the moments when quite new sense,
To meet some need as novel,
Springs up in the brain: it inspired resource:
—"Nor advance nor retreat but—grovel!"

And slowly, surely, never a whit
Relaxing the steady tension
Of eye-stare which binds man to beast,—
By an inch and inch declension,

Sank Donald sidewise down and down:
Till flat, breast upwards, lying
At his six-foot length, no corpse more still,
—"If he cross me! The trick 's worth trying."

Minutes were an eternity;
But a new sense was created
In the stag's brain too; he resolves! Slow, sure,
With eye-stare unabated,

Feelingly he extends a foot
Which tastes the way ere it touches
Earth's solid and just escapes man's soft,
Nor hold of the same unclutches

Till its fellow foot, light as a feather whisk,

Lands itself no less finely:
So a mother removes a fly from the face
Of her babe asleep supinely.

And now 't is the haunch and hind-foot's turn
—That 's hard: can the beast quite raise it?
Yes, traversing half the prostrate length,
His hoof-tip does not graze it.

Just one more lift! But Donald, you see,
Was sportsman first, man after:
A fancy lightened his caution through,
—He wellnigh broke into laughter:

"It were nothing short of a miracle!
Unrivalled, unexampled—
All sporting feats with this feat matched
Were down and dead and trampled!"

The last of the legs as tenderly
Follows the rest: or never
Or now is the time! His knife in reach,
And his right-hand loose—how clever!

For this can stab up the stomach's soft,
While the left-hand grasps the pastern.
A rise on the elbow, and—now 's the time
Or never: this turn 's the last turn!

I shall dare to place myself by God
Who scanned—for he does—each feature
Of the face thrown up in appeal to him
By the agonizing creature.

Nay, I hear plain words: "Thy gift brings this!"
Up he sprang, back he staggered,
Over he fell, and with him our friend
—At following game no laggard.

Yet he was not dead when they picked next day
From the gully's depth the wreck of him;
His fall had been stayed by the stag beneath
Who cushioned and saved the neck of him.

But the rest of his body—why, doctors said,
Whatever could break was broken;
Legs, arms, ribs, all of him looked like a toast
In a tumbler of port-wine soaken.

"That your life is left you, thank the stag!"
Said they when—the slow cure ended—
They opened the hospital-door, and thence
—Strapped, spliced, main fractures mended,

And minor damage left wisely alone,—
Like an old shoe clouted and cobbled,
Out—what went in a Goliath wellnigh,—
Some half of a David hobbled.

"You must ask an alms from house to house:
Sell the stag's head for a bracket,
With its grand twelve tines—I 'd buy it myself—
And use the skin for a jacket!"

He was wiser, made both head and hide
His win-penny: hands and knees on,
Would manage to crawl—poor crab—by the roads
In the misty stalking-season.

And if he discovered a bothy like this,
Why, harvest was sure: folk listened.
He told his tale to the lovers of Sport:
Lips twitched, cheeks glowed, eyes glistened.

And when he had come to the close, and spread
His spoils for the gazers' wonder,
With "Gentlemen, here 's the skull of the stag
I was over, thank God, not under!"—

The company broke out in applause;
"By Jingo, a lucky cripple!
Have a munch of grouse and a hunk of bread,
And a tug, besides, at our tipple!"

And "There 's my pay for your pluck!" cried This,
"And mine for your jolly story!"
Cried That, while T' other—but he was drunk—
Hiccupped "A trump, a Tory!"

I hope I gave twice as much as the rest;
For, as Homer would say, "within grate
Though teeth kept tongue," my whole soul growled,
"Rightly rewarded,—Ingrate!"

SOLOMON AND BALKIS

Solomon King of the Jews and the Queen of Sheba, Balkis,
Talk on the ivory throne, and we well may conjecture their talk is
Solely of things sublime: why else has she sought Mount Zion,
Climbed the six golden steps, and sat betwixt lion and lion?

She proves him with hard questions: before she has reached the middle
He smiling supplies the end, straight solves them riddle by riddle;
Until, dead-beaten at last, there is left no spirit in her,
And thus would she close the game whereof she was first beginner:

"O wisest thou of the wise, world's marvel and wellnigh monster,
One crabbed question more to construe or vulgo conster!
Who are those, of all mankind, a monarch of perfect wisdom
Should open to, when they knock at spheteron do—that 's, his dome?"

The King makes tart reply: "Whom else but the wise his equals
Should he welcome with heart and voice?—since, king though he be, such weak walls
Of circumstance—power and pomp—divide souls each from other
That whoso proves kingly in craft I needs must acknowledge my brother.

"Come poet, come painter, come sculptor, come builder—whate'er his condition,
Is he prime in his art? We are peers! My insight has pierced the partition
And hails—for the poem, the picture, the statue, the building—my fellow!
Gold 's gold though dim in the dust: court-polish soon turns it yellow.

"But tell me in turn, O thou to thy weakling sex superior,
That for knowledge hast travelled so far yet seemest nowhit the wearier,—
Who are those, of all mankind, a queen like thyself, consummate
In wisdom, should call to her side with an affable 'Up hither, come, mate'?"

"The Good are my mates—how else? Why doubt it?" the Queen upbridled:
"Sure even above the Wise,—or in travel my eyes have idled,—
I see the Good stand plain: be they rich, poor, shrewd, or simple,
If Good they only are.... Permit me to drop my wimple!"

And, in that bashful jerk of her body, she—peace, thou scoffer!—
Jostled the King's right-hand stretched courtously help to proffer,
And so disclosed a portent: all unaware the Prince eyed
The Ring which bore the Name—turned outside now from inside!

The truth-compelling Name!—and at once, "I greet the Wise—oh,
Certainly welcome such to my court—with this proviso:
The building must be my temple, my person stand forth the statue,
The picture my portrait prove, and the poem my praise—you cat, you!"

But Solomon nonplussed? Nay! "Be truthful in turn!" so bade he:

"See the Name, obey its hest!" And at once subjoins the lady,
—"Provided the Good are the young, men strong and tall and proper,
Such servants I straightway enlist,—which means" ... But the blushes stop her.

"Ah, Soul," the Monarch sighed, "that wouldst soar yet ever crawlest,
How comes it thou canst discern the greatest yet choose the smallest,
Unless because heaven is far, where wings find fit expansion,
While creeping on all-fours suits, suffices the earthly mansion?

"Aspire to the Best! But which? There are Bests and Bests so many,
With a habitat each for each, earth's Best as much Best as any!
On Lebanon roots the cedar—soil lofty, yet stony and sandy—
While hyssop, of worth in its way, on the wall grows low but handy.

"Above may the Soul spread wing, spurn body and sense beneath her;
Below she must condescend, to plodding unbuoyed by ether.
In heaven I yearn for knowledge, account all else inanity;
On earth I confess an itch for the praise of fools—that 's Vanity.

"It is naught, it will go, it can never presume above to trouble me;
But here,—why, it toys and tickles and teases, howe'er I redouble me
In a doggedest of endeavors to play the indifferent. Therefore,
Suppose we resume discourse? Thou hast travelled thus far: but wherefore?"

"Solely for Solomon's sake, to see whom earth styles Sagest?"
Through her blushes laughed the Queen. "For the sake of a Sage? The gay jest!
On high, be communion with Mind—there, Body concerns not Balkis:
Down here,—do I make too bold? Sage Solomon,—one fool's small kiss!"

CRISTINA AND MONALDESCHI

Ah, but how each loved each, Marquis!
Here 's the gallery they trod
Both together, he her god,
She his idol,—lend your rod,
Chamberlain!—ay, there they are—"Quis
Separabit?"—plain those two
Touching words come into view,
Apposite for me and you:

Since they witness to incessant
Love like ours: King Francis, he—
Diane the adored one, she—
Prototypes of you and me.
Everywhere is carved her Crescent
With his Salamander-sign—

Flame-fed creature: flame benign
To itself or, if malign,

Only to the meddling curious,
—So, be warned, Sir! Where 's my head?
How it wanders! What I said
Merely meant—the creature, fed
Thus on flame, was scarce injurious
Save to fools who woke its ire,
Thinking fit to play with fire.
'T is the Crescent you admire?

Then, be Diane! I 'll be Francis.
Crescents change,—true!—wax and wane,
Woman-like: male hearts retain
Heat nor, once warm, cool again.
So, we figure—such our chance is—
I as man and you as ... What?
Take offence? My Love forgot
He plays woman, I do not?

I—the woman? See my habit,
Ask my people! Anyhow,
Be we what we may, one vow
Binds us, male or female. Now,—
Stand, Sir! Read! "Quis separabit?"
Half a mile of pictured way
Past these palace-walls to-day
Traversed, this I came to say.

You must needs begin to love me;
First I hated, then, at best,
—Have it so!—I acquiesced;
Pure compassion did the rest.
From below thus raised above me,
Would you, step by step, descend,
Pity me, become my friend,
Like me, like less, loathe at end?

That 's the ladder's round you rose by!
That—my own foot kicked away,
Having raised you: let it stay,
Serve you for retreating? Nay.
Close to me you climbed: as close by,
Keep your station, though the peak
Reached proves somewhat bare and bleak!
Woman 's strong if man is weak.

Keep here, loving me forever!
Love's look, gesture, speech, I claim:
Act love, lie love, all the same—
Play as earnest were our game!
Lonely I stood long: 't was clever
When you climbed, before men's eyes,
Spurned the earth and scaled the skies,
Gained my peak and grasped your prize.

Here you stood, then, to men's wonder;
Here you tire of standing? Kneel!
Cure what giddiness you feel,
This way! Do your senses reel?
Not unlikely! What rolls under?
Yawning death in yon abyss
Where the waters whirl and hiss
Round more frightful peaks than this.

Should my buffet dash you thither ...
But be sage! No watery grave
Needs await you: seeming brave
Kneel on safe, dear timid slave!
You surmised, when you climbed hither,
Just as easy were retreat
Should you tire, conceive unmeet
Longer patience at my feet?

Me as standing, you as stooping,—
Who arranged for each the pose?
Lest men think us friends turned foes,
Keep the attitude you chose!
Men are used to this same grouping—
I and you like statues seen.
You and I, no third between,
Kneel and stand! That makes the scene.

Mar it—and one buffet ... Pardon!
Needless warmth—wise words in waste!
'T was prostration that replaced
Kneeling, then? A proof of taste.
Crouch, not kneel, while I mount guard on
Prostrate love—become no waif,
No estray to waves that chafe
Disappointed—love 's so safe!

Waves that chafe? The idlest fancy!
Peaks that scare? I think we know
Walls enclose our sculpture: so

Grouped, we pose in Fontainebleau.
Up now! Wherefore hesitancy?
Arm in arm and cheek by cheek,
Laugh with me at waves and peak!
Silent still? Why, pictures speak.

See, where Juno strikes Ixion,
Primatice speaks plainly! Pooh—
Rather, Florentine Le Roux!
I 've lost head for who is who—
So it swims and wanders! Fie on
What still proves me female! Here,
By the staircase!—for we near
That dark "Gallery of the Deer."

Look me in the eyes once! Steady!
Are you faithful now as erst
On that eve when we two first
Vowed at Avon, blessed and cursed
Faith and falsehood? Pale already?
Forward! Must my hand compel
Entrance—this way? Exit—well,
Somehow, somewhere. Who can tell?

What if to the selfsame place in
Rustic Avon, at the door
Of the village church once more,
Where a tombstone paves the floor
By that holy-water basin
You appealed to—"As, below.
This stone hides its corpse, e'en so
I your secrets hide"? What ho!

Friends, my four! You, Priest, confess him!
I have judged the culprit there:
Execute my sentence! Care
For no mail such cowards wear!
Done, Priest? Then, absolve and bless him!
Now—you three, stab thick and fast,
Deep and deeper! Dead at last?
Thanks, friends—Father, thanks! Aghast?

What one word of his confession
Would you tell me, though I lured
With that royal crown abjured
Just because its bars immured
Love too much? Love burst compression,
Fled free, finally confessed

All its secrets to that breast
Whence ... let Avon tell the rest!

MARY WOLLSTONECRAFT AND FUSELI

Oh, but is it not hard, Dear?
Mine are the nerves to quake at a mouse:
If a spider drops I shrink with fear:
I should die outright in a haunted house;
While for you—did the danger dared bring help—
From a lion's den I could steal his whelp,
With a serpent round me, stand stock-still,
Go sleep in a churchyard,—so would will
Give me the power to dare and do
Valiantly—just for you!

Much amiss in the head, Dear,
I toil at a language, tax my brain
Attempting to draw—the scratches here!
I play, play, practise, and all in vain:
But for you—if my triumph brought you pride,
I would grapple with Greek Plays till I died,
Paint a portrait of you—who can tell?
Work my fingers off for your "Pretty well:"
Language and painting and music too,
Easily done—for you!

Strong and fierce in the heart, Dear,
With—more than a will—what seems a power
To pounce on my prey, love outbroke here
In flame devouring and to devour.
Such love has labored its best and worst
To win me a lover; yet, last as first,
I have not quickened his pulse one beat,
Fixed a moment's fancy, bitter or sweet:
Yet the strong fierce heart's love's labor's due,
Utterly lost, was—you!

ADAM, LILITH, AND EVE

One day, it thundered and lightened.
Two women, fairly frightened,
Sank to their knees, transformed, transfixed,
At the feet of the man who sat betwixt;

And "Mercy!" cried each—"if I tell the truth
Of a passage in my youth!"

Said This: "Do you mind the morning
I met your love with scorning?
As the worst of the venom left my lips,
I thought, 'If, despite this lie, he strips
The mask from my soul with a kiss—I crawl
His slave,—soul, body, and all!'"

Said That: "We stood to be married;
The priest, or some one, tarried;
'If Paradise-door prove locked?' smiled you.
I thought, as I nodded, smiling too,
'Did one, that 's away, arrive—nor late
Nor soon should unlock Hell's gate!'"

It ceased to lighten and thunder.
Up started both in wonder,
Looked round and saw that the sky was clear,
Then laughed "Confess you believed us, Dear!"
"I saw through the joke!" the man replied
They re-seated themselves beside.

IXION

High in the dome, suspended, of Hell, sad triumph, behold us!
Here the revenge of a God, there the amends of a Man.
Whirling forever in torment, flesh once mortal, immortal
Made—for a purpose of hate—able to die and revive,
Pays to the uttermost pang, then, newly for payment replenished,
Doles out—old yet young—agonies ever afresh;
Whence the result above me: torment is bridged by a rainbow,—
Tears, sweat, blood,—each spasm, ghastly once, glorified now.
Wrung, by the rush of the wheel ordained my place of reposing,
Off in a sparklike spray,—flesh become vapor through pain,—
Flies the bestowment of Zeus, soul's vaunted bodily vesture,
Made that his feats observed gain the approval of Man,—
Flesh that he fashioned with sense of the earth and the sky and the ocean,
Framed should pierce to the star, fitted to pore on the plant,—
All, for a purpose of hate, re-framed, re-fashioned, re-fitted,
Till, consummate at length,—lo, the employment of sense!
Pain's mere minister now to the soul, once pledged to her pleasure—
Soul, if untrammelled by flesh, unapprehensive of pain!
Body, professed soul's slave, which serving beguiled and betrayed her,
Made things false seem true, cheated through eye and through ear,

Lured thus heart and brain to believe in the lying reported,—
Spurn but the trait'rous slave, uttermost atom, away,
What should obstruct soul's rush on the real, the only apparent?
Say I have erred,—how else? Was I Ixion or Zeus?
Foiled by my senses I dreamed; I doubtless awaken in wonder:
This proves shine, that—shade? Good was the evil that seemed?
Shall I, with sight thus gained, by torture be taught I was blind once?
Sisuphos, teaches thy stone—Tantalos, teaches thy thirst
Aught which unaided sense, purged pure, less plainly demonstrates?
No, for the past was dream: now that the dreamers awake,
Sisuphos scouts low fraud, and to Tantalos treason is folly.
Ask of myself, whose form melts on the murderous wheel,
What is the sin which throe and throe prove sin to the sinner!
Say the false charge was true,—thus do I expiate, say,
Arrogant thought, word, deed,—mere man who conceited me godlike,
Sat beside Zeus, my friend—knelt before Heré, my love!
What were the need but of pitying power to touch and disperse it,
Film-work—eye's and ear's—all the distraction of sense?
How should the soul not see, not hear,—perceive and as plainly
Render, in thought, word, deed, back again truth—not a lie?
"Ay, but the pain is to punish thee!" Zeus, once more for a pastime,
Play the familiar, the frank! Speak and have speech in return!
I was of Thessaly king, there ruled and a people obeyed me:
Mine to establish the law, theirs to obey it or die:
Wherefore? Because of the good to the people, because of the honor
Thence accruing to me, king, the king's law was supreme.
What of the weakling, the ignorant criminal? Not who, excuseless,
Breaking my law braved death, knowing his deed and its due—
Nay, but the feeble and foolish, the poor transgressor, of purpose
No whit more than a tree, born to erectness of bole,
Palm or plane or pine, we laud if lofty, columnar—
Loathe if athwart, askew,—leave to the axe and the flame!
Where is the vision may penetrate earth and beholding acknowledge
Just one pebble at root ruined the straightness of stem?
Whose fine vigilance follows the sapling, accounts for the failure,
—Here blew wind, so it bent: there the snow lodged, so it broke?
Also the tooth of the beast, bird's bill, mere bite of the insect
Gnawed, gnarled, warped their worst: passive it lay to offence.
King—I was man, no more: what I recognized faulty I punished,
Laying it prone: be sure, more than a man had I proved,
Watch and ward o'er the sapling at birthtime had saved it, nor simply
Owned the distortion's excuse,—hindered it wholly: nay, more—
Even a man, as I sat in my place to do judgment, and pallid
Criminals passing to doom shuddered away at my foot,
Could I have probed through the face to the heart, read plain a repentance,
Crime confessed fools' play, virtue ascribed to the wise,
Had I not stayed the consignment to doom, not dealt the renewed ones
Life to retraverse the past, light to retrieve the misdeed?

Thus had I done, and thus to have done much more it behooves thee,
Zeus who madest man—flawless or faulty, thy work!
What if the charge were true, as thou mouthest,—Ixion the cherished
Minion of Zeus grew vain, vied with the godships and fell,
Forfeit through arrogance? Stranger! I clothed, with the grace of our human,
Inhumanity—gods, natures I likened to ours.
Man among men I had borne me till gods forsooth must regard me
—Nay, must approve, applaud, claim as a comrade at last.
Summoned to enter their circle, I sat—their equal, how other?
Love should be absolute love, faith is in fulness or naught.
"I am thy friend, be mine!" smiled Zeus: "If Heré attract thee,"
Blushed the imperial cheek, "then—as thy heart may suggest!"
Faith in me sprang to the faith, my love hailed love as its fellow,
"Zeus, we are friends—how fast! Heré, my heart for thy heart!"
Then broke smile into fury of frown, and the thunder of "Hence, fool!"
Then through the kiss laughed scorn "Limbs or a cloud was to clasp?"
Then from Olumpos to Erebos, then from the rapture to torment,
Then from the fellow of gods—misery's mate, to the man!
—Man henceforth and forever, who lent from the glow of his nature
Warmth to the cold, with light colored the black and the blank.
So did a man conceive of your passion, you passion-protesters!
So did he trust, so love—being the truth of your lie!
You to aspire to be Man! Man made you who vainly would ape him:
You are the hollowness, he—filling you, falsifies void.
Even as—witness the emblem, Hell's sad triumph suspended,
Born of my tears, sweat, blood—bursting to vapor above—
Arching my torment, an iris ghostlike startles the darkness,
Cold white—jewelry quenched—justifies, glorifies pain.
Strive, mankind, though strife endure through endless obstruction,
Stage after stage, each rise marred by as certain a fall!
Baffled forever—yet never so baffled but, e'en in the baffling,
When Man's strength proves weak, checked in the body or soul,
Whatsoever the medium, flesh or essence,—Ixion's
Made for a purpose of hate,—clothing the entity Thou,
—Medium whence that entity strives for the Not-Thou beyond it,
Fire elemental, free, frame unencumbered, the All,—
Never so baffled but—when, on the verge of an alien existence,
Heartened to press, by pangs burst to the infinite Pure,
Nothing is reached but the ancient weakness still that arrests strength,
Circumambient still, still the poor human array,
Pride and revenge and hate and cruelty—all it has burst through,
Thought to escape,—fresh formed, found in the fashion it fled,
Never so baffled but—when Man pays the price of endeavor,
Thunderstruck, downthrust, Tartaros-doomed to the wheel,—
Then, ay, then, from the tears and sweat and blood of his torment,
E'en from the triumph of Hell, up let him look and rejoice!
What is the influence, high o'er Hell, that turns to a rapture
Pain—and despair's murk mist blends in a rainbow of hope?

What is beyond the obstruction, stage by stage though it baffle?
Back must I fall, confess "Ever the weakness I fled"?
No, for beyond, far, far is a Purity all-unobstructed!
Zeus was Zeus—not Man: wrecked by his weakness, I whirl.
Out of the wreck I rise—past Zeus to the Potency o'er him!
I—to have hailed him my friend! I—to have clasped her—my love!
Pallid birth of my pain,—where light, where light is, aspiring
Thither I rise, whilst thou—Zeus, keep the godship and sink!

JOCHANAN HAKKADOSH

"This now, this other story makes amends
And justifies our Mishna," quoth the Jew
Aforesaid. "Tell it, learnedest of friends!"

A certain morn broke beautiful and blue
O'er Schiphaz city, bringing joy and mirth,
—So had ye deemed; while the reverse was true,

Since one small house there gave a sorrow birth
In such black sort that, to each faithful eye,
Midnight, not morning settled on the earth.

How else, when it grew certain thou wouldst die,
Our much-enlightened master, Israel's prop,
Eximious Jochanan Ben Sabbathai?

Old, yea, but, undiminished of a drop,
The vital essence pulsed through heart and brain;
Time left unsickled yet the plenteous crop

On poll and chin and cheek, whereof a skein
Handmaids might weave—hairs silk-soft, silver-white,
Such as the wool-plant's; none the less in vain

Had Physic striven her best against the spite
Of fell disease: the Rabbi must succumb;
And, round the couch whereon in piteous plight

He lay a-dying, scholars,—awe-struck, dumb
Throughout the night-watch,—roused themselves and spoke
One to the other: "Ere death's touch benumb

"His active sense,—while yet 'neath Reason's yoke
Obedient toils his tongue,—befits we claim
The fruit of long experience, bid this oak

"Shed us an acorn which may, all the same,
Grow to a temple-pillar,—dear that day!—
When Israel's scattered seed finds place and name

"Among the envious nations. Lamp us, pray,
Thou the Enlightener! Partest hence in peace?
Hailest without regret—much less, dismay—

"The hour of thine approximate release
From fleshly bondage soul hath found obstruct?
Calmly envisagest the sure increase

"Of knowledge? Eden's tree must hold unplucked
Some apple, sure, has never tried thy tooth,
Juicy with sapience thou hast sought, not sucked?

"Say, does age acquiesce in vanished youth?
Still towers thy purity above—as erst—
Our pleasant follies? Be thy last word—truth!"

The Rabbi groaned; then, grimly, "Last as first
The truth speak I—in boyhood who began
Striving to live an angel, and, amerced

"For such presumption, die now hardly man.
What have I proved of life? To live, indeed,
That much I learned: but here lies Jochanan

"More luckless than stood David when, to speed
His fighting with the Philistine, they brought
Saul's harness forth: whereat, 'Alack, I need

"Armor to arm me, but have never fought
With sword and spear, nor tried to manage shield,
Proving arms' use, as well-trained warrior ought,

"'Only a sling and pebbles can I wield!'
So he: while I, contrariwise, 'No trick
Of weapon helpful on the battlefield

"'Comes unfamiliar to my theoric:
But, bid me put in practice what I know,
Give me a sword—it stings like Moses' stick,

"'A serpent I let drop apace.' E'en so,
I,—able to comport me at each stage
Of human life as never here below

"Man played his part,—since mine the heritage
Of wisdom carried to that perfect pitch,
Ye rightly praise,—I, therefore, who, thus sage,

"Could sure act man triumphantly, enrich
Life's annals, with example how I played
Lover, Bard, Soldier, Statist,—(all of which

"Parts in presentment failing, cries invade
The world's ear—'Ah, the Past, the pearl-gift thrown
To hogs, time's opportunity we made

"'So light of, only recognized when flown!
Had we been wise!')—-in fine, I—wise enough,—
What profit brings me wisdom never shown

"Just when its showing would from each rebuff
Shelter weak virtue, threaten back to bounds
Encroaching vice, tread smooth each track too rough

"For youth's unsteady footstep, climb the rounds
Of life's long ladder, one by slippery one,
Yet make no stumble? Me hard fate confounds

"With that same crowd of wailers I outrun
By promising to teach another cry
Of more hilarious mood than theirs, the sun

"I look my last at is insulted by.
What cry,—ye ask? Give ear on every side!
Witness yon Lover! 'How entrapped am I!

"'Methought, because a virgin's rose-lip vied
With ripe Khubbezleh's, needs must beauty mate
With meekness and discretion in a bride:

"'Bride she became to me who wail—too late—
Unwise I loved!' That 's one cry. 'Mind 's my gift:
I might have loaded me with lore, full weight

"'Pressed down and running over at each rift
O' the brain-bag where the famished clung and fed.
I filled it with what rubbish!—would not sift

"'The wheat from chaff, sound grain from musty—shed
Poison abroad as oft as nutriment—
And sighing say but as my fellows said,

"'Unwise I learned!' That 's two. 'In dwarfs-play spent
Was giant's prowess: warrior all unversed
In war's right waging, I struck brand, was lent

"'For steel's fit service, on mere stone—and cursed
Alike the shocked limb and the shivered steel,
Seeing too late the blade's true use which erst

"How was I blind to! My cry swells the peal—
Unwise I fought!' That 's three. But wherefore waste
Breath on the wailings longer? Why reveal

"A root of bitterness whereof the taste
Is noisome to Humanity at large?
First we get Power, but Power absurdly placed

"In Folly's keeping, who resigns her charge
To Wisdom when all Power grows nothing worth:
Bones marrowless are mocked with helm and targe

"When, like your Master's, soon below the earth
With worms shall warfare only be. Farewell,
Children! I die a failure since my birth!"

"Not so!" arose a protest, as, pell-mell,
They pattered from his chamber to the street,
Bent on a last resource. Our Targums tell

That such resource there is. Put case, there meet
The Nine Points of Perfection—rarest chance—
Within some saintly teacher whom the fleet

Years, in their blind implacable advance,
O'ertake before fit teaching born of these
Have magnified his scholars' countenance,—

If haply folk compassionating please
To render up—according to his store,
Each one—a portion of the life he sees

Hardly worth saving when 't is set before
Earth's benefit should the Saint, Hakkadosh,
Favored thereby, attain to full fourscore—

If such contribute (Scoffer, spare thy "Bosh!")
A year, a month, a day, an hour—to eke
Life out,—in him away the gift shall wash

That much of ill-spent time recorded, streak
The twilight of the so-assisted sage
With a new sunrise: truth, though strange to speak!

Quick to the doorway, then, where youth and age,
All Israel, thronging, waited for the last
News of the loved one. "'T is the final stage:

"Art's utmost done, the Rabbi's feet tread fast
The way of all flesh!" So announced that apt
Olive-branch Tsaddik: "Yet, O Brethren, east

"No eye to earthward! Look where heaven has clapped
Morning's extinguisher—yon ray-shot robe
Of sun-threads—on the constellation mapped

"And mentioned by our Elders,—yea, from Job
Down to Satam,—as figuring forth—what?
Perpend a mystery! Ye call it Dob,

"'The Bear': I trow, a wiser name than that
Were Aish—'The Bier': a corpse those four stars hold,
Which—are not those Three Daughters weeping at

"Banoth? I judge so: list while I unfold
The reason. As in twice twelve hours this Bier
Goes and returns, about the east-cone rolled,

"So may a setting luminary here
Be rescued from extinction, rolled anew
Upon its track of labor, strong and clear,

"About the Pole—that Salem, every Jew
Helps to build up when thus he saves some Saint
Ordained its architect. Ye grasp the clue

"To all ye seek? The Rabbi's lamp-flame faint
Sinks: would ye raise it? Lend then life from yours,
Spare each his oil-drop! Do I need acquaint

"The Chosen how self-sacrifice ensures
Tenfold requital?—urge ye emulate
The fame of those Old Just Ones death procures

"Such praise for, that 't is now men's sole debate
Which of the Ten, who volunteered at Rome
To die for glory to our Race, was great

"Beyond his fellows? Was it thou—the comb
Of iron carded, flesh from bone, away,
While thy lips sputtered through their bloody foam

"Without a stoppage (O brave Akiba!)
'Hear, Israel, our Lord God is One'? Or thou,
Jischab?—who smiledst, burning, since there lay,

"Burning along with thee, our Law! I trow,
Such martyrdom might tax flesh to afford:
While that for which I make petition now,

"To what amounts it? Youngster, wilt thou hoard
Each minute of long years thou look'st to spend
In dalliance with thy spouse? Hast thou so soared,

"Singer of songs, all out of sight of friend
And teacher, warbling like a woodland bird,
There 's left no Selah, 'twixt two psalms, to lend

"Our late-so-tuneful quirist? Thou, averred
The fighter born to plant our lion-flag
Once more on Zion's mount,—doth all-unheard,

"My pleading fail to move thee? Toss some rag
Shall stanch our wound, some minute never missed
From swordsman's lustihood like thine! Wilt lag

"In liberal bestowment, show close fist
When open palm we look for,—thou, wide-known
For statecraft? whom, 't is said, and if thou list,

"The Shah himself would seat beside his throne,
So valued were advice from thee" ... But here
He stopped short: such a hubbub! Not alone

From those addressed, but far as well as near
The crowd brought into clamor: "Mine, mine, mine—
Lop from my life the excrescence, never fear!

"At me thou lookedst, markedst me! Assign
To me that privilege of granting life—
Mine, mine!" Then he: "Be patient! I combine

"The needful portions only, wage no strife
With Nature's law nor seek to lengthen out
The Rabbi's day unduly. 'T is the knife

"I stop,—would eat its thread too short. About
As much as helps life last the proper term,
The appointed Fourscore,—that I crave, and scout

"A too-prolonged existence. Let the worm
Change at fit season to the butterfly!
And here a story strikes me, to confirm

"This judgment. Of our worthies, none ranks high
As Perida who kept the famous school:
None rivalled him in patience: none! For why?

"In lecturing it was his constant rule,
Whatever he expounded, to repeat
—Ay, and keep on repeating, lest some fool

"Should fail to understand him fully—(feat
Unparalleled, Uzzean!)—do ye mark?—
Five hundred times! So might he entrance beat

"For knowledge into howsoever dark
And dense the brain-pan. Yet it happed, at close
Of one especial lecture, not one spark

"Of light was found to have illumed the rows
Of pupils round their pedagogue. 'What, still
Impenetrable to me? Then—here goes!'

"And for a second time he sets the rill
Of knowledge running, and five hundred times
More re-repeats the matter—and gains nil.

"Out broke a voice from heaven: 'Thy patience climbs
Even thus high. Choose! Wilt thou, rather, quick
Ascend to bliss—or, since thy zeal sublimes

"'Such drudgery, will thy back still bear its crick,
Bent o'er thy class,—thy voice drone spite of drouth,—
Five hundred years more at thy desk wilt stick?'

"'To heaven with me!' was in the good man's mouth,
When all his scholars—cruel-kind were they!—
Stopped utterance, from East, West, North and South,

"Rending the welkin with their shout of 'Nay—
No heaven as yet for our instructor! Grant
Five hundred years on earth for Perida!'

"And so long did he keep instructing! Want
Our Master no such misery! I but take
Three months of life marital. Ministrant

"Be thou of so much, Poet! Bold I make,
Swordsman, with thy frank offer!—and conclude,
Statist, with thine! One year,—ye will not shake

"My purpose to accept no more. So rude?
The very boys and girls, forsooth, must press
And proffer their addition? Thanks! The mood

"Is laudable, but I reject, no less,
One month, week, day of life more. Leave my gown,
Ye overbold ones! Your life's gift, you guess,

"Were good as any? Rudesby, get thee down!
Set my feet free, or fear my staff! Farewell,
Seniors and saviors, sharers of renown

"With Jochanan henceforward!" Straightway fell
Sleep on the sufferer; who awoke in health,
Hale everyway, so potent was the spell.

O the rare Spring-time! Who is he by stealth
Approaches Jochanan?—embowered that sits
Under his vine and figtree 'mid the wealth

Of garden-sights and sounds, since intermits
Never the turtle's coo, nor stays nor stints
The rose her smell. In homage that befits

The musing Master, Tsaddik, see, imprints
A kiss on the extended foot, low bends
Forehead to earth, then, all-obsequious, hints

"What if it should be time? A period ends—
That of the Lover's gift—his quarter-year
Of lustihood: 't is just thou make amends,

"Return that loan with usury: so, here
Come I, of thy Disciples delegate,
Claiming our lesson from thee. Make appear

"Thy profit from experience! Plainly state
How men should Love!" Thus he: and to him thus
The Rabbi: "Love, ye call it?—rather, Hate!

"What wouldst thou? Is it needful I discuss
Wherefore new sweet wine, poured in bottlescaked
With old strong wine's deposit, offers us

"Spoilt liquor we recoil from, thirst-unslaked?
Like earth-smoke from a crevice, out there wound—
Languors and yearnings: not a sense but ached

"Weighed on by fancied form and feature, sound
Of silver word and sight of sunny smile:
No beckoning of a flower-branch, no profound

"Purple of noon-oppression, no light wile
O' the West wind, but transformed itself till—brief—
Before me stood the phantasy ye style

"Youth's love, the joy that shall not come to grief,
Born to endure, eternal, unimpaired
By custom the accloyer, time the thief.

"Had Age's hard cold knowledge only spared
That ignorance of Youth! But now the dream,
Fresh as from Paradise, alighting fared

"As fares the pigeon, finding what may seem
Her nest's safe hollow holds a snake inside
Coiled to enclasp her. See, Eve stands supreme

"In youth and beauty! Take her for thy bride!
What Youth deemed crystal, Age finds out was dew
Morn set a-sparkle, but which noon quick dried

"While Youth bent gazing at its red and blue
Supposed perennial,—never dreamed the sun
Which kindled the display would quench it too.

"Graces of shape and color—every one
With its appointed period of decay
When ripe to purpose! 'Still, these dead and done,

"'Survives the woman-nature—the soft sway
Of undefinable omnipotence
O'er our strong male-stuff, we of Adam's clay.'

"Ay, if my physics taught not why and whence
The attraction! Am I like the simple steer
Who, from his pasture lured inside the fence,

"Where yoke and goad await him, holds that mere
Kindliness prompts extension of the hand
Hollowed for barley, which drew near and near

"His nose—in proof that, of the hornèd band,
The farmer best affected him? Beside,
Steer, since his calfhood, got to understand

"Farmers a many in the world so wide
Were ready with a handful just as choice
Or choicer—maize and cummin, treats untried.

"Shall I wed wife, and all my days rejoice
I gained the peacock? 'Las me, round I look,
And lo—'With me thou wouldst have blamed no voice

"'Like hers that daily deafens like a rook:
I am the phœnix!'—'I, the lark, the dove,
—The owl,' for aught knows he who blindly took

"Peacock for partner, while the vale, the grove,
The plain held bird-mates in abundance. There!
Youth, try fresh capture! Age has found out Love

"Long ago. War seems better worth man's care.
But leave me! Disappointment finds a balm
Haply in slumber." "This first step o' the stair

"To knowledge fails me, but the victor's palm
Lies on the next to tempt him overleap
A stumbling-block. Experienced, gather calm,

"Thou excellence of Judah, cured by sleep
Which ushers in the Warrior, to replace
The Lover! At due season I shall reap

"Fruit of my planting!" So, with lengthened face,
Departed Tsaddik: and three moons more waxed
And waned, and not until the summer-space

Waned likewise, any second visit taxed
The Rabbi's patience. But at three months' end
Behold, supine beneath a rock, relaxed

The sage lay musing till the noon should spend
Its ardor. Up comes Tsaddik, who but he,
With "Master, may I warn thee, nor offend,

"That time comes round again? We look to see
Sprout from the old branch—not the youngling twig—
But fruit of sycamine: deliver me,

"To share among my fellows, some plump fig
Juicy as seedy! That same man of war,
Who, with a scantling of his store, made big

"Thy starveling nature, caused thee, safe from scar,
To share his gains by long acquaintanceship
With bump and bruise and all the knocks that are

"Of battle dowry,—he bids loose thy lip,
Explain the good of battle! Since thou know'st,
Let us know likewise! Fast the moments slip,

"More need that we improve them!"—"Ay, we boast,
We warriors in our youth, that with the sword
Man goes the swiftliest to the uttermost—

"Takes the straight way through lands yet unexplored
To absolute Right and Good,—may so obtain
God's glory and man's weal too long ignored,

"Too late attained by preachments all in vain—
The passive process. Knots get tangled worse
By toying with: does cut cord close again?

"Moreover there is blessing in the curse
Peace-praisers call war. What so sure evolves
All the capacities of soul, proves nurse

"Of that self-sacrifice in men which solves
The riddle—Wherein differs Man from beast?
Foxes boast cleverness and courage wolves:

"Nowhere but in mankind is found the least
Touch of an impulse 'To our fellows—good
I' the highest!—not diminished but increased

"'By the condition plainly understood
—Such good shall be attained at price of hurt
I' the highest to ourselves!' Fine sparks that brood

"Confusedly in Man, 't is war bids spurt
Forth into flame: as fares the meteor-mass,
Whereof no particle but holds inert

"Some seed of light and heat, however crass
The enclosure, yet avails not to discharge
Its radiant birth before there come to pass

"Some push external,—strong to set at large
Those dormant fire-seeds; whirl them in a trice
Through heaven, and light up earth from marge to marge:

"Since force by motion makes—what erst was ice—
Crash into fervency and so expire,
Because some Djinn has hit on a device

"For proving the full prettiness of fire!
Ay, thus we prattle—young: but old—why, first,
Where 's that same Right and Good—(the wise inquire)—

"So absolute, it warrants the outburst
Of blood, tears, all war's woeful consequence,
That comes of the fine flaring? Which plague cursed

"The more your benefited Man—offence,
Or what suppressed the offender? Say it did—
Show us the evil cured by violence,

"Submission cures not also! Lift the lid
From the maturing crucible, we find
Its slow sure coaxing-out of virtue, hid

"In that same meteor-mass, hath uncombined
Those particles and, yielding for result
Gold, not mere flame, by so much leaves behind

"The heroic product. E'en the simple cult
Of Edom's children wisely bids them turn
Cheek to the smiter with 'Sic Jesus vult.'

"Say there 's a tyrant by whose death we earn
Freedom, and justify a war to wage:
Good!—were we only able to discern

"Exactly how to reach and catch and cage
Him only and no innocent beside!
Whereas the folk whereon war wreaks its rage

"—How shared they his ill-doing? Far and wide
The victims of our warfare strew the plain,
Ten thousand dead, whereof not one but died

"In faith that vassals owed their suzerain
Life: therefore each paid tribute—honest soul—
To that same Right and Good ourselves are fain

"To call exclusively our end. From bole
(Since ye accept in me a sycamine)
Pluck, eat, digest a fable—yea, the sole

"Fig I afford you! 'Dost thou dwarf my vine?'
(So did a certain husbandman address
The tree which faced his field.) 'Receive condign

"'Punishment, prompt removal by the stress
Of axe I forthwith lay unto thy root!'
Long did he hack and hew, the root no less

"As long defied him, for its tough strings shoot
As deep down as the boughs above aspire:
All that he did was—shake to the tree's foot

"Leafage and fruitage, things we most require
For shadow and refreshment: which good deed
Thoroughly done, behold the axe-haft tires

"His hand, and he desisting leaves unfreed
The vine he hacked and hewed for. Comes a frost,
One natural night's work, and there 's little need

"Of hacking, hewing: lo, the tree 's a ghost!
Perished it starves, black death from topmost bough
To farthest-reaching fibre! Shall I boast

"My rough work—warfare—helped more? Loving, now—
That, by comparison, seems wiser, since
The loving fool was able to avow

"He could effect his purpose, just evince
Love's willingness,—once 'ware of what she lacked,
His loved one,—to go work for that, nor wince

"At self-expenditure: he neither hacked
Nor hewed, but when the lady of his field
Required defence because the sun attacked,

"He, failing to obtain a fitter shield,
Would interpose his body, and so blaze,
Blest in the burning. Ah, were mine to wield

"The intellectual weapon—poet-lays,—
How preferably had I sung one song
Which ... but my sadness sinks me: go your ways!

"I sleep out disappointment." "Come along,
Never lose heart! There 's still as much again
Of our bestowment left to right the wrong

"Done by its earlier moiety—explain
Wherefore, who may! The Poet's mood comes next.
Was he not wishful the poetic vein

"Should pulse within him? Jochanan, thou reck'st
Little of what a generous flood shall soon
Float thy clogged spirit free and unperplexed

"Above dry dubitation! Song 's the boon
Shall make amends for my untoward mistake
That Joshua-like thou couldst bid sun and moon—

"Fighter and Lover,—which for most men make
All they descry in heaven,—stand both stock-still
And lend assistance. Poet shalt thou wake!"

Autumn brings Tsaddik. "Ay, there speeds the rill
Loaded with leaves: a scowling sky, beside:
The wind makes olive-trees up yonder hill

"Whiten and shudder—symptoms far and wide
Of gleaning-time's approach; and glean good store
May I presume to trust we shall, thou tried

"And ripe experimenter! Three months more
Have ministered to growth of Song: that graft
Into thy sterile stock has found at core

"Moisture, I warrant, hitherto unquaffed
By boughs, however florid, wanting sap
Of prose-experience which provides the draught

"Which song-sprouts, wanting, wither: vain we tap
A youngling stem all green and immature;
Experience must secrete the stuff, our hap

"Will be to quench Man's thirst with, glad and sure
That fancy wells up through corrective fact:
Missing which test of truth, though flowers allure

"The goodman's eye with promise, soon the pact
Is broken, and 'tis flowers—mere words—he finds
When things—that's fruit—he looked for. Well, once cracked

"The nut, how glad my tooth the kernel grinds!
Song may henceforth boast substance! Therefore, hail
Proser and poet, perfect in both kinds!

"Thou from whose eye hath dropped the envious scale
Which hides the truth of things and substitutes
Deceptive show, unaided optics fail

"To transpierce,—hast entrusted to the lute's
Soft but sure guardianship some unrevealed
Secret shall lift mankind above the brutes

"As only knowledge can?" "A fount unsealed"
(Sighed Jochanan) "should seek the heaven in leaps
To die in dew-gems—not find death, congealed

"By contact with the cavern's nether deeps,
Earth's secretest foundation where, enswathed
In dark and fear, primeval mystery sleeps—

"Petrific fount wherein my fancies bathed
And straight turned ice. My dreams of good and fair
In soaring upwards had dissolved, unscathed

"By any influence of the kindly air,
Singing, as each took flight, 'The Future—that's
Our destination, mists turn rainbows there,

"'Which sink to fog, confounded in the flats
O' the Present! Day's the song-time for the lark,
Night for her music boasts but owls and bats.

"'And what's the Past but night—the deep and dark
Ice-spring I speak of, corpse-thicked with its drowned
Dead fancies which no sooner touched the mark

"'They aimed at—fact—than all at once they found
Their film-wings freeze, henceforth unfit to reach
And roll in ether, revel—robed and crowned

"'As truths confirmed by falsehood all and each—
Sovereign and absolute and ultimate!
Up with them, skyward, Youth, ere Age impeach

"'Thy least of promises to reinstate
Adam in Eden!' Sing on, ever sing,
Chirp till thou burst!—the fool cicada's fate,

"Who holds that after Summer next comes Spring,
Than Summer's self sun-warmed, spice-scented more.
Fighting was better! There, no fancy-fling

"Pitches you past the point was reached of yore
By Samsons, Abners, Joabs, Judases,
The mighty men of valor who, before

"Our little day, did wonders none profess
To doubt were fable and not fact, so trust
By fancy-flights to emulate much less.

"Were I a Statesman, now! Why, that were just
To pinnacle my soul, mankind above,
A-top the universe: no vulgar lust

"To gratify—fame, greed, at this remove
Looked down upon so far—or overlooked
So largely, rather—that mine eye should rove

"World-wide and rummage earth, the many-nooked,
Yet find no unit of the human flock
Caught straying but straight comes back hooked and crooked

"By the strong shepherd who, from out his stock
Of aids proceeds to treat each ailing fleece,
Here stimulate to growth, curtail and dock

"There, baldness or excrescence,—that, with grease,
This, with up-grubbing of the bristly patch
Born of the tick-bite. How supreme a peace

"Steals o'er the Statist,—while, in wit, a match
For shrewd Ahithophel, in wisdom ... well,
His name escapes me—somebody, at watch

"And ward, the fellow of Ahithophel
In guidance of the Chosen!"—at which word
Eyes closed and fast asleep the Rabbi fell.

"Cold weather!" shivered Tsaddik. "Yet the hoard
Of the sagacious ant shows garnered grain,
Ever abundant most when fields afford

"Least pasture, and alike disgrace the plain
Tall tree and lowly shrub. 'T is so with us
Mortals: our age stores wealth ye seek in vain

"While busy youth culls just what we discuss
At leisure in the last days: and the last
Truly are these for Jochanan, whom thus

"I make one more appeal to! Thine amassed
Experience, now or never, let escape
Some portion of! For I perceive aghast

"The end approaches, while they jeer and jape,
These sons of Shimei: 'Justify your boast!
What have ye gained from Death by twelve months' rape?'

"Statesman, what cure hast thou for—least and most—
Popular grievances? What nostrum, say,
Will make the Rich and Poor, expertly dosed,

"Forget disparity, bid each go gay,
That, with his bauble,—with his burden, this?
Propose an alkahest shall melt away

"Men's lacquer, show by prompt analysis
Which is the metal, which the make-believe,
So that no longer brass shall find, gold miss

"Coinage and currency? Make haste, retrieve
The precious moments, Master!" Whereunto
There snarls an "Ever laughing in thy sleeve,

"Pert Tsaddik? Youth indeed sees plain a clue
To guide man where life's wood is intricate:
How shall he fail to thrid its thickest through

"When every oak-trunk takes the eye? Elate
He goes from hole to brushwood, plunging finds—
Smothered in briers—that the small's the great!

"All men are men: I would all minds were minds!
Whereas 't is just the many's mindless mass
That most needs helping: laborers and hinds

"We legislate for—not the cultured class
Which law-makes for itself nor needs the whip
And bridle,—proper help for mule and ass,

"Did the brutes know! In vain our statesmanship
Strives at contenting the rough multitude:
Still the ox cries "T is me thou shouldst equip

"'With equine trappings!' or, in humbler mood,
'Cribful of corn for me! and, as for work—
Adequate rumination o'er my food!'

"Better remain a Poet! Needs it irk
Such an one if light, kindled in his sphere,
Fail to transfuse the Mizraim cold and murk

"Round about Goshen? Though light disappear,
Shut inside,—temporary ignorance
Got outside of, lo, light emerging clear

"Shows each astonished starer the expanse
Of heaven made bright with knowledge! That's the way,
The only way—I see it at a glance—

"To legislate for earth! As poet ... Stay!
What is ... I would that ... were it ... I had been ...
O sudden change, as if my arid clay

"Burst into bloom!" ... "A change indeed, I ween,
And change the last!" sighed Tsaddik as he kissed
The closing eyelids. "Just as those serene

"Princes of Night apprised me! Our acquist
Of life is spent, since corners only four
Hath Aisch, and each in turn was made desist

"In passage round the Pole (O Mishna's lore—
Little it profits here!) by strenuous tug
Of friends who eked out thus to full fourscore

"The Rabbi's years. I see each shoulder shrug!
What have we gained? Away the Bier may roll!
To-morrow, when the Master's grave is dug,

"In with his body I may pitch the scroll
I hoped to glorify with, text and gloss,
My Science of Man's Life: one blank's the whole!

"Love, war, song, statesmanship—no gain, all loss,
The stars' bestowment! We on our return
To-morrow merely find—not gold but dross,

"The body not the soul. Come, friends, we learn
At least thus much by our experiment—
That—that ... well, find what, whom it may concern!"

But next day through the city rumors went
Of a new persecution; so, they fled
All Israel, each man,—this time,—from his tent,

Tsaddik among the foremost. When, the dread
Subsiding, Israel ventured back again
Some three months after, to the cave they sped

Where lay the Sage,—a reverential train!
Tsaddik first enters. "What is this I view?
The Rabbi still alive? No stars remain

"Of Aisch to stop within their courses. True,
I mind me, certain gamesome boys must urge
Their offerings on me: can it be—one threw

"Life at him and it stuck? There needs the scourge
To teach that urchin manners! Prithee, grant
Forgiveness if we pretermit thy dirge

"Just to explain no friend was ministrant,
This time, of life to thee! Some jackanapes,
I gather, has presumed to foist his scant

"Scurvy unripe existence—wilding grapes
Grass-green and sorrel-sour—on that grand wine,
Mighty as mellow, which, so fancy shapes

"May fitly image forth this life of thine
Fed on the last low fattening lees—condensed
Elixir, no milk-mildness of the vine!

"Rightly with Tsaddik wert thou now incensed
Had he been witting of the mischief wrought
When, for elixir, verjuice he dispensed!"

And slowly woke,—like Shushan's flower besought
By over-curious handling to unloose
The curtained secrecy wherein she thought

Her captive bee, 'mid store of sweets to choose,
Would loll, in gold pavilioned lie unteased,
Sucking on, sated never,—whose, O whose

Might seem that countenance, uplift, all eased
Of old distraction and bewilderment,
Absurdly happy? "How ye have appeased

"The strife within me, bred this whole content,
This utter acquiescence in my past,
Present and future life,—by whom was lent

"The power to work this miracle at last,—
Exceeds my guess. Though—ignorance confirmed
By knowledge sounds like paradox, I cast

"Vainly about to tell you—fitlier termed—
Of calm struck by encountering opposites,
Each nullifying either! Henceforth wormed

"From out my heart is every snake that bites
The dove that else would brood there: doubt, which kills
With hiss of 'What if sorrows end delights?'

"Fear which stings ease with 'Work the Master wills!'
Experience which coils round and strangles quick
Each hope with 'Ask the Past if hoping skills

"'To work accomplishment, or proves a trick
Wiling thee to endeavor! Strive, fool, stop
Nowise, so live, so die—that's law! why kick

"'Against the pricks?' All out-wormed! Slumber, drop
Thy films once more and veil the bliss within!
Experience strangle hope? Hope waves a-top

"Her wings triumphant! Come what will, I win,
Whoever loses! Every dream's assured
Of soberest fulfilment. Where's a sin

"Except in doubting that the light, which lured
The unwary into darkness, meant no wrong
Had I but marched on bold, nor paused immured

"By mists I should have pressed through, passed along
My way henceforth rejoicing? Not the boy's
Passionate impulse he conceits so strong,

"Which, at first touch, truth, bubble-like, destroys,—
Not the man's slow conviction 'Vanity
Of vanities—alike my griefs and joys!'

"Ice!—thawed (look up) each bird, each insect by—
(Look round) by all the plants that break in bloom,
(Look down) by every dead friend's memory

"That smiles 'Am I the dust within my tomb?'
Not either, but both these—amalgam rare—
Mix in a product, not from Nature's womb,

"But stuff which He the Operant—who shall dare
Describe His operation?—strikes alive
And thaumaturgic. I nor know nor care

"How from this tohu-bohu—hopes which dive,
And fears which soar—faith, ruined through and through
By doubt, and doubt, faith treads to dust?—revive

"In some surprising sort,—as see, they do!—
Not merely foes no longer but fast friends.
What does it mean unless—O strange and new

"Discovery!—this life proves a wine-press—blends
Evil and good, both fruits of Paradise,
Into a novel drink which—who intends

"To quaff, must bear a brain for ecstasies
Attempered, not this all-inadequate
Organ which, quivering within me, dies

"—Nay, lives!—what, how,—too soon, or else too late—
I was—I am" ... ("He babbleth!" Tsaddik mused)
"O Thou Almighty, who canst reinstate

"Truths in their primal clarity, confused
By man's perception, which is man's and made
To suit his service,—how, once disabused

"Of reason which sees light half shine half shade,
Because of flesh, the medium that adjusts
Purity to his visuals, both an aid

"And hindrance,—how to eyes earth's air encrusts,
When purged and perfect to receive truth's beam
Pouring itself on the new sense it trusts

"With all its plenitude of power,—how seem
The intricacies now, of shade and shine,
Oppugnant natures—Right and Wrong, we deem

"Irreconcilable? O eyes of mine,
Freed now of imperfection, ye avail
To see the whole sight, nor may uncombine

"Henceforth what, erst divided, caused you quail—
So huge the chasm between the false and true,
The dream and the reality! All hail,

"Day of my soul's deliverance—day the new,
The never-ending! What though every shape
Whereon I wreaked my yearning to pursue

"Even to success each semblance of escape
From my own bounded self to some all-fair
All-wise external fancy, proved a rape

"Like that old giant's, feigned of fools—on air,
Not solid flesh? How otherwise? To love—
That lesson was to learn not here—but there—

"On earth, not here! 'Tis there we learn,—there prove
Our parts upon the stuff we needs must spoil,
Striving at mastery, there bend above

"The spoiled clay potsherds, many a year of toil
Attests the potter tried his hand upon,
Till sudden he arose, wiped free from soil

"His hand, cried 'So much for attempt—anon
Performance! Taught to mould the living vase,
What matter the cracked pitchers dead and gone?'

"Could I impart and could thy mind embrace
The secret, Tsaddik!" "Secret none to me!"
Quoth Tsaddik, as the glory on the face

Of Jochanan was quenched. "The truth I see
Of what that excellence of Judah wrote,
Doughty Halaphta. This a case must be

"Wherein, though the last breath, have passed the throat,
So that 'The man is dead' we may pronounce,
Yet is the Ruach—(thus do we denote

"The imparted Spirit)—in no haste to bounce
From its entrusted Body,—some three days
Lingers ere it relinquish to the pounce

"Of hawk-clawed Death his victim. Further says
Halaphta, 'Instances have been, and yet
Again may be, when saints, whose earthly ways

"'Tend to perfection, very nearly get
To heaven while still on earth: and, as a fine
Interval shows where waters pure have met

"'Waves brackish, in a mixture, sweet with brine,
That's neither sea nor river but a taste
Of both—so meet the earthly and divine

"'And each is either.' Thus I hold him graced—
Dying on earth, half inside and half out,
Wholly in heaven, who knows? My mind embraced

"Thy secret, Jochanan, how dare I doubt?
Follow thy Ruach, let earth, all it can,
Keep of the leavings!" Thus was brought about

The sepulture of Rabbi Jochanan:
Thou hast him,—sinner-saint, live-dead, boy-man,—
Schiphaz, on Bendimir, in Farzistan!

NOTE.—This story can have no better authority than that of the treatise, existing dispersedly in fragments, of Rabbinical writing, מֹשֶׁךְ שֶׁל דבים בדים, *from which I might have helped myself more liberally. Thus, instead of the simple reference to "Moses' stick,"—but what if I make amends by attempting three illustrations, when some thirty might be composed on the same subject, equally justifying that pithy proverb* ממשה עד משה לא קם במשה.

I

Moses the Meek was thirty cubits high,
The staff he strode with—thirty cubits long;
And when he leapt, so muscular and strong
Was Moses that his leaping neared the sky
By thirty cubits more: we learn thereby
He reached full ninety cubits—am I wrong?—
When, in a fight slurred o'er by sacred song,
With staff outstretched he took a leap to try
The just dimensions of the giant Og.
And yet he barely touched—this marvel lacked
Posterity to crown earth's catalogue
Of marvels—barely touched—to be exact—
The giant's ankle-bone, remained a frog
That fain would match an ox in stature: fact!

II

And this same fact has met with unbelief!
How saith a certain traveller? "Young, I chanced
To come upon an object—if thou canst,
Guess me its name and nature! 'Twas, in brief,
White, hard, round, hollow, of such length, in chief,
—And this is what especially enhanced
My wonder—that it seemed, as I advanced,
Never to end. Bind up within thy sheaf
Of marvels, this—Posterity! I walked
From end to end,—four hours walked I, who go
A goodly pace,—and found—I have not balked
Thine expectation, Stranger? Ay or No?—
'T was but Og's thighbone, all the while, I stalked
Alongside of: respect to Moses, though!

III

Og's thighbone—if ye deem its measure strange,
Myself can witness to much length of shank
Even in birds. Upon a water's bank
Once halting, I was minded to exchange
Noon heat for cool. Quoth I, "On many a grange
I have seen storks perch—legs both long and lank:
Yon stork's must touch the bottom of this tank,
Since on its top doth wet no plume derange
Of the smooth breast. I'll bathe there!" "Do not so!"
Warned me a voice from heaven. "A man let drop
His axe into that shallow rivulet—
As thou accountest—seventy years ago:
It fell and fell and still without a stop
Keeps falling, nor has reached the bottom yet."

NEVER THE TIME AND THE PLACE

Never the time and the place
And the loved one all together!
This path—how soft to pace!
This May—what magic weather!
Where is the loved one's face?
In a dream that loved one's face meets mine,
But the house is narrow, the place is bleak
Where, outside, rain and wind combine

With a furtive ear, if I strive to speak,
With a hostile eye at my flushing cheek,
With a malice that marks each word, each sign!
O enemy sly and serpentine,
Uncoil thee from the waking man!
Do I hold the Past
Thus firm and fast
Yet doubt if the Future hold I can?
This path so soft to pace shall lead
Through the magic of May to herself indeed!
Or narrow if needs the house must be,
Outside are the storms and strangers: we—
Oh, close, safe, warm sleep I and she,
—I and she!

PAMBO

Suppose that we part (work done, comes play)
With a grave tale told in crambo
—As our hearty sires were wont to say—
Whereof the hero is Pambo?

Do you happen to know who Pambo was?
Nor I—but this much have heard of him:
He entered one day a college-class,
And asked—was it so absurd of him?—

"May Pambo learn wisdom ere practise it?
In wisdom I fain would ground me:
Since wisdom is centred in Holy Writ,
Some psalm to the purpose expound me!"

"That psalm," the Professor smiled, "shall be
Untroubled by doubt which dirtieth
Pellucid streams when an ass like thee
Would drink there—the Nine-and-thirtieth.

"Verse First: I said I will look to my ways
That I with my tongue offend not.
How now? Why stare? Art struck in amaze?
Stop, stay! The smooth line hath an end knot!

"He's gone!—disgusted my text should prove
Too easy to need explaining?
Had he waited, the blockhead might find I move
To matter that pays remaining!"

Long years went by, when—"Ha, who's this?
Do I come on the restive scholar
I had driven to Wisdom's goal, I wis,
But that he slipped the collar?

"What? Arms crossed, brow bent, thought-immersed?
A student indeed! Why scruple
To own that the lesson proposed him first
Scarce suited so apt a pupil?

"Come back! From the beggarly elements
To a more recondite issue
We pass till we reach, at all events,
Some point that may puzzle.... Why 'pish' you?"

From the ground looked piteous up the head:
"Daily and nightly, Master,
Your pupil plods through that text you read,
Yet gets on never the faster.

"At the selfsame stand,—now old, then young!
I will look to my ways—were doing
As easy as saying!—that I with my tongue
Offend not—and 'scape pooh-poohing

"From sage and simple, doctor and dunce?
Ah, nowise! Still doubts so muddy
The stream I would drink at once,—but once!
That—thus I resume my study!"

Brother, brother, I share the blame,
Arcades sumus ambo!
Darkling, I keep my sunrise-aim,
Lack not the critic's flambeau,
And look to my ways, yet, much the same,
Offend with my tongue—like Pambo!

Robert Browning – A Short Biography

He is the equal of any Victorian Poet that could be mentioned. However, Browning continues to be in the shadow of Tennyson, Arnold, Hopkins, Morris and many others.

Robert Browning was born on May 7th, 1812 in Walworth in the parish of Camberwell, London. He was baptized on June 14th, 1812, at Lock's Fields Independent Chapel, York Street, Walworth.

Browning's early years were certainly very interesting. His mother was an excellent pianist and a very devout evangelical Christian. His father, who worked as a clerk at the Bank of England, was also an artist, scholar, antiquarian, and collector of books and pictures. Indeed, he amassed more than 6,000 volumes of rare books including works in Greek, Hebrew, Latin, French, Italian, and Spanish. For the young and curious Browning, it was a wonderful resource, added to which his father was a guiding force in his education.

Many accounts attest that Browning was already proficient at reading and writing by the age of five. He is said to have been a bright but anxious student and to have studied and learnt Latin, Greek, and French by the time he was fourteen. From fourteen to sixteen he was educated at home, tutored in music, drawing, dancing, and horsemanship. Certainly, language and the arts were two areas the young Browning both absorbed and pushed himself towards.

At the age of twelve he wrote a volume of Byronic verse he called Incondita, which his parents attempted to have published. The attempts were unsuccessful and, disappointed, Browning destroyed the work.

In 1825, a cousin gave Browning a collection of Percy Bysshe Shelley's poetry; Browning was so enamored with the poems that he asked for the rest of Shelley's works for his thirteenth birthday. In fact, Browning then went the extra mile, declaring himself to be both a vegetarian and an atheist in honour of his hero.

Intriguingly it seems that the rejection of his first volume didn't dim his appreciation of other poets, but it appears to have stopped him writing any poems between the ages of thirteen and twenty.

In 1828, Browning enrolled at the newly-opened University of London. He was uncomfortable with the experience and he soon left, anxious to read and absorb at his own pace.

His education which, overall is notably rambling and lacks a structure that many of his artistic contemporaries enjoyed, i.e. excellent public schooling and then a degree at Oxford or Cambridge, may present many of his critics with ammunition to criticize, but alternatively his hap-hazard education certainly contributed to many of the references that baffled both critics and his audience, but they tellingly show the breath and scale of what he could turn words too. What others would call obscure references were, to Browning, remarkably obvious.

Browning's early career was very promising. His long poem Pauline (of which only a fragment was ever finished and published) brought him to the attention of the Pre-Raphaelite master Dante Gabriel Rossetti and his difficult Paracelsus (published in 1835) was warmly admired by both Dickens and Wordsworth.

In the 1830s he met the actor William Macready and was encouraged to develop and turn his talents to the stage by writing verse drama. But these plays, including Strafford, which ran for five nights in 1837, and those contained within the Bells and Pomegranates series, were, for the most part, unsuccessful.

During this period Browning began to discover that his real talents lay in taking a single character and allowing that character to discover more about himself by revealing further personal aspects of himself in his speeches; the dramatic monologue. The techniques he developed through this—especially the use of diction, rhythm, and symbol—are regarded as his most important contribution to poetry. They would later influence such major poets of the 20th Century as Ezra Pound, T. S. Eliot, and Robert Frost.

By 1840, with the publication of Sordello, the tide turned somewhat. Many thought he was being deliberately obscure, opaque beyond measure and his poetry for the next decade or so was not eagerly acquired or talked about.

As Browning attempted to rehabilitate his career he began a relationship with Elizabeth Barrett in 1845. He had read her poems and, being totally charmed by their quality, was determined to meet her. The poetess was better known than the younger Browning but suffered from a debilitating illness and was also subject to the harsh behaviour of her over-bearing father. Nevertheless, the new couple were soon inseparable.

Her father, as he did with any of his children that married, disinherited her. Despite this she had some money from her own resources and sensing that the best outcome for both the relationship and her own health was to move abroad the couple did just that. After a private marriage at St Marylebone Parish Church, in September 1846, they journeyed to Europe to honeymoon in Paris.

Their new life now took them to Italy, first to Pisa and a little later to Florence. There they absorbed life and one another.

But in the short term the literary assault on Browning's work did not let up. He was now criticized by such patrician writers as Charles Kingsley for his abandonment of England for foreign lands. Browning could do little to answer these attacks except to compose with his pen and continue with his poetical journey.

The Browning's were well respected, and even famous. Elizabeth health began to improve, she grew stronger and in 1849, at the age of 43, between four miscarriages, she gave birth to a son, Robert Wiedeman Barrett Browning, whom they nicknamed "Penini" or "Pen",

Intriguingly despite his growing reputation and return to form as a poet he was more often than not known as 'Elizabeth Barrett's husband'.

Work flowed from his pen that was to ensure his reputation as one of England's leading poets. When his collection Men and Women was published in 1855 it contained some of his finest lines. It was dedicated to Elizabeth. Life had begun to smile handsome rewards upon the Brownings.

Victorian society was very much taken with all things spiritualist. It was not enough to have command of much of the globe through Empire, they wished to know and explore wherever they could. The spirit world beckoned their interest. Browning dissented from this view believing it was all a hoax and a fraud. Elizabeth, however, was inclined to believe and this caused several disagreements between the couple.

They attended a séance by Daniel Dunglas Home, in July 1855. (Home was a famous and clamored after Scottish physical medium with the reported ability to levitate and speak with the dead). It is said that during this séance a spirit face materialised. Home then claimed it was the face of Browning's son who had died in infancy. Browning seized the 'materialisation' which turned out to be Home's bare foot. Browning had never lost a son in infancy.

After the séance, Browning wrote an angry letter to The Times, in which he said: "the whole display of hands, spirit utterances etc., was a cheat and imposture."

The Browning's time in Italy were immensely rewarding years for both their personal and professional lives. Browning encouraged her to include Sonnets from the Portuguese in her published works, these beautiful poems are undoubtedly one of the highlights of English love poetry.

Elizabeth had become quite politicised during these years. Engrossed in Italian politics (which was continuing to slowly re-unify the country), she issued a small volume of political poems entitled Poems before Congress (1860) most of which were written to express her sympathy with the Italian cause after the earlier outbreak of The Second Italian Independence War in 1859. In England they caused uproar. Conservative magazines such as Blackwood's and the Saturday Review labelled her a fanatic. She dedicated the book to her husband.

But in 1861 tragedy struck.

The couple had spent the winter of 1860–61 in Rome when Elizabeth's health deteriorated again and they returned to Florence in early June. However, these turned out to be her final weeks. Only morphine would now still the pain. She died in Browning's arms on June 29th, 1861. Browning said that she died "smilingly, happily, and with a face like a girl's .... Her last word was .... "Beautiful".

Her burial took place in the nearby Protestant English Cemetery of Florence. The local people were deeply saddened, and shops closed their doors in grief and respect.

Browning and their son were obviously devastated. Unable to bear being in Florence without Elizabeth they soon returned to London to live at 19 Warwick Crescent, Maida Vale.

As he re-integrated himself back into the London literary scene he began to finally receive the proper praise, respect and reputation that his works deserved.

Browning went on to publish Dramatis Personæ (1864), and The Ring and the Book (1868–1869). The latter, based on an "old yellow book" which told of a seventeenth-century Italian murder trial, received wide and generous critical acclaim. Although by now he was in the twilight of a long and prolific career, that had achieved some notable ups and downs, he was respected and indeed renowned for his talents and works.

In 1878, he revisited Italy for the first time since Elizabeth's death. He would return there on several further occasions but never to Florence.

Such was the esteem he was held in that The Browning Society was founded in 1881. Although he had never obtained a degree (something that set him apart from many other Victorian poets) he was now awarded honorary degrees from Oxford University in 1882 and then the University of Edinburgh in 1884.

In 1887, Browning produced the major work of his later years, Parleyings with Certain People of Importance in Their Day. Browning now spoke with his own voice as he engaged in a series of dialogues with long-forgotten figures of literary, artistic, and philosophic history. Unfortunately, both the critics and public were completely baffled by this.

On April 7th, 1889 Browning attended a dinner party at the home of his friend, the artist Rudolf Lehmann. The highlight of which was a recording made on a wax cylinder on an Edison cylinder phonograph. On the recording, which still exists, Browning recites part of How They Brought the Good News from Ghent to Aix, and can even be heard apologising when he forgets the words.

The recording was first played in 1890 on the anniversary of his death, at a gathering of his admirers, it was said to be the first time anyone's voice 'had been heard from beyond the grave'.

His last work Asolando: Fancies and Facts (1889), returned to his brief and concise lyric verse that was so popular. It was published on the day of his death on December 12th, 1889, Robert Browning was at his son's home Ca' Rezzonico in Venice.

He was buried in Poets' Corner in Westminster Abbey; his grave lies immediately adjacent to that of Alfred Tennyson.

Among the many who have publicly acknowledged their literary debt to him are Henry James, Oscar Wilde, George Bernard Shaw, G. K. Chesterton, Ezra Pound, Jorge Luis Borges, and Vladimir Nabokov.

Robert Browning - A Concise Bibliography

Here follows a list of the plays and poetry volumes published during his lifetime. Poems of particular worth are noted from within those volumes.

Pauline: A Fragment of a Confession (1833)
Paracelsus (1835)
Strafford (play) (1837)
Sordello (1840)
Bells and Pomegranates No. I: Pippa Passes (play) (1841)
        The Year's at the Spring
Bells and Pomegranates No. II: King Victor and King Charles (play) (1842)
Bells and Pomegranates No. III: Dramatic Lyrics (1842)
        Porphyria's Lover
        Soliloquy of the Spanish Cloister
        My Last Duchess
        The Pied Piper of Hamelin
        Count Gismond
        Johannes Agricola in Meditation
Bells and Pomegranates No. IV: The Return of the Druses (play) (1843)
Bells and Pomegranates No. V: A Blot in the 'Scutcheon (play) (1843)
Bells and Pomegranates No. VI: Colombe's Birthday (play) (1844)
Bells and Pomegranates No. VII: Dramatic Romances and Lyrics (1845)
        The Laboratory
        How They Brought the Good News from Ghent to Aix
        The Bishop Orders His Tomb at Saint Praxed's Church
        The Lost Leader
        Home Thoughts from Abroad